A Note From Denise Renner

The Word of God is so powerful in our lives. It is essential that every person spend time with God and study His Word in order to stay spiritually strong in these last days.

This study guide corresponds to my *TIME With Denise Renner* TV program by the same title that can be viewed at **deniserenner.org**. My desire is that through these lessons, you find the encouragement and freedom in Christ that you need. I believe the Holy Spirit is going to speak to you through the words you read in this study tool and that as you begin to use it, you will be *propelled* into the abundant life God has planned for you. I encourage you to make the effort to receive all He has for you and all He wants to do in you — it will definitely be worth it!

Whether you have walked with the Lord a long time or have just begun to follow Him, there is so much He wants to give you from His Word. He sees where you are, and He wants to meet you there.

> Therefore do not worry about tomorrow, for tomorrow
> will worry about its own things.
> Sufficient for the day is its own trouble.
> — Matthew 6:34

Your sister and friend in Jesus Christ,

Denise Renner

The Armor of God

Copyright © 2024 by Denise Renner
1814 W. Tacoma St.
Broken Arrow, Oklahoma 74012-1406

Published by Rick Renner Ministries
www.renner.org

ISBN 13: 978-1-6675-0640-1

ISBN 13 eBook: 978-1-6675-0641-8

TOPIC

Activate the Belt of Truth

SCRIPTURES

1. **John 8:32** — "And you shall know the truth, and the truth shall make you free."
2. **Ephesians 6:12** — For we do not wrestle against flesh and blood, but against principalities, against powers, against the rulers of the darkness of this age, against spiritual hosts of wickedness in the heavenly places.
3. **1 Corinthians 10:13** — No temptation has overtaken you except such as is common to man; but God is faithful, who will not allow you to be tempted beyond what you are able, but with the temptation will also make the way of escape, that you may be able to bear it.
4. **Ephesians 6:13,14** — Therefore take up the whole armor of God, that you may be able to withstand in the evil day, and having done all, to stand. Stand therefore, having girded your waist with truth, having put on the breastplate of righteousness.
5. **2 Corinthians 13:5** — Examine yourselves as to whether you are in the faith. Test yourselves. Do you not know yourselves, that Jesus Christ is in you? — unless indeed you are disqualified.
6. **1 Peter 1:18,19** — Knowing that you were not redeemed with corruptible things, like silver or gold, from your aimless conduct received by tradition from your fathers, but with the precious blood of Christ, as of a lamb without blemish and without spot.

SYNOPSIS

The apostle Paul was in prison when he wrote the book of Ephesians. And in Ephesians 6, he describes the spiritual armor available to every born-again believer. The first weapon is Truth — God's Word — bound like a belt around the waist. God's Word is the most important element of the Christian walk. Your body is the very temple of the Holy Spirit, the place where God dwells. When knowledge of God's Word becomes heart knowledge, it changes us. We are not our own. We were bought with the price of the precious blood of Jesus Christ!

The emphasis of this lesson:

The belt of truth, which is the Word of God, is a vital part of our God-given spiritual weapons and the most important aspect of our intimate walk with God. We must utilize these weapons that are at our disposal to successfully overcome the onslaught of the enemy against us.

The Belt of Truth

It was under the inspiration of the Holy Spirit that the apostle Paul wrote the book of Ephesians. While locked away in a Roman prison and awaiting trial, Paul likely observed the armor that was worn by the Roman soldiers who were guarding him. He used the First Century battle dress of the Roman soldier as a metaphor for God's spiritual armor that is made available to every born-again child of God.

The first piece of armor Paul wrote about is the belt of truth. In Ephesians 6:14 Paul stated, "Stand therefore, having girded your waist with truth…." Many people today often say, "I have *my* truth." But what is truth? Truth is the Word of God — the Bible. No other "truth" is able to conquer the assaults of the enemy against our lives. Only God's Word contains the power to defeat every weapon the devil has formed against us.

Anyone can turn on the news and quickly observe the problems in our world today. We are living in challenging times, but God has not called us to simply identify the problem. We are called to be more than conquerors (*see* Romans 8:37). But how do we not allow problems from the outside world to defeat us or dictate how we live our lives? Jesus said in John 8:32, "And you shall know the truth, and the truth shall make you free." The answer is in finding the truth that sets us free.

The belt of truth is the first piece of armor mentioned by Paul because it is foundational. It is on the belt that the Roman soldier hung his other weapons, including his dagger, sword, and protective apron. Similarly, it is on *our* spiritual belt of truth — the written Word of God — that we secure *our* other spiritual weapons that God has given us. The Word of God is the most important weapon in our arsenal.

We Do Not Wrestle Against Flesh and Blood

The devil has weapons he tries to use against every believer. For example, when we are faced with temptation, he tries to make us believe that no one has ever been tempted as badly as we are being tempted. He tries to isolate us and manipulate circumstances to validate his lies. John 8:44 describes the devil as "a liar and the father of it."

But First Corinthians 10:13 declares, "No temptation has overtaken you except such is as common to man; but God is faithful, who will not allow you to be tempted beyond what you are able, but with the temptation will also make the way of escape, that you may be able to bear it." The truth is that every temptation that you have ever faced (or ever will face) is common to man. So that temptation is not unique; millions of others have faced that same temptation. In addition, God promises you the way of escape.

We are in a battle, but the battle is not against flesh and blood. We are not battling against a spouse, a child, a friend, or an employer. Ephesians 6:12 clearly states, "For we do not wrestle against flesh and blood, but against principalities, against powers, against the rulers of the darkness of this age, against spiritual hosts of wickedness in the heavenly places." The devil has waged a supernatural war against every child of God, but God has provided the armor for us to overcome every attack.

Ephesians 6:13 instructs us to "take up the whole armor of God, that you may be able to withstand in the evil day, and having done all, to stand." God's armor is available to us, but we must *take it up*. Again, the first piece of armor addressed is the belt of truth. In verse 14, Paul said, "...Having girded your waist with truth...."

How important is our "waist"? The waist is often referred to as our "core," and it's important to exercise to strengthen it, as a strong core will benefit the entire body. Similarly, Truth — the Word of God — will strengthen us spiritually. God's Word is the most important weapon upon which all of the other weapons depend.

You Are the Temple of the Holy Spirit

It's important to understand that the physical body of a believer is not the same as the body of a person who is not born again. First Corinthians 6:19 and 20 emphasizes, "...Do you not know that your body is the temple of the

Holy Spirit who is in you, whom you have from God, and you are not your own? For you were bought at a price; therefore glorify God in your body and in your spirit, which are God's."

If you are born-again, your body is the very house in which the Holy Spirit dwells. Regardless of the size of your natural body, you are filled completely with the presence of God! The apostle John declared, "…He who is in you is greater than he who is in the world" (1 John 4:4). And in Second Corinthians 13:5, Paul asked, "…Do you not know yourselves, that Jesus Christ is in you?" Your body is a temple — a dwelling place for God!

We do not belong to ourselves — we belong to God, and this truth must become more than just head knowledge; it must become *heart* knowledge. When we simply "know" (head knowledge) that the Holy Spirit lives inside us, we continue to allow ourselves to be controlled by our emotions or our bodies or negative thoughts contrary to the Word. But when we apply what we are learning from God's Word to our daily lives it becomes heart knowledge, and heart knowledge changes the way we act, and it changes our attitude.

In the Old Testament, men would construct places for God's presence to dwell. In the times of David, the Ark of the Covenant — the place of God's dwelling — would be placed in the Holy of Holies in the Temple. Once a year, one priest was allowed to enter the Holy of Holies on behalf of the people. But when Jesus went to the Cross and the veil of the Temple was torn in two, He opened the way for you and me to become the very dwelling place of God!

When the belt of truth is wrapped around our waist — when we abide in the Word of God — even if the enemy hurls lies against us, we can say, "No. I may not be perfect in my emotions or my mind or my body, but God lives in my spirit and my spirit is perfect because that is where He dwells." The One who dwells inside us is greater than anything in this world.

Bought With a Price

First Peter 1:18 and 19 says, "…You were not redeemed with corruptible things, like silver or gold, from your aimless conduct received by tradition from your fathers, but with the precious blood of Christ, as of a lamb without blemish and without spot." As Jesus was flogged by the Roman soldiers and as He hung on the Cross and His blood was poured out, that blood was the very price that bought you and me. It bought us back from the slavery of the enemy that held us bound by sickness, depression, and shame. His blood bought us back from a vicious slave master whose plan was to abuse and destroy us. But Jesus bought us out of slavery and delivered us from the slave market by pouring out His precious blood on the Cross! We are not orphans, and we do not belong to ourselves. We belong to God, and we are now His children.

In Psalm 18:2, David wrote, "The Lord is my rock, and my fortress, and my deliverer; my God, my strength, in whom I will trust; my buckler…." The "buckler" referred to a shield, and during times of war, a soldier bearing a buckler was designated to stand between the enemy and the king. If the enemy armies shot arrows at the king, it would first encounter the soldier carrying the buckler. Picture the Lord standing between you and every fiery arrow from the devil! The Lord is your Great Protector — your Buckler!

And in Psalm 23, David declared, "The Lord is my Shepherd…." Why? Because the Lord feeds, protects, and teaches His sheep. We are His sheep because He bought us with His blood and we belong to Him. Your body is the very temple in which God now dwells, and as you acknowledge and declare, "Greater is He that is in me than he that is in the world" (1 John 4:4), you are utilizing your weaponry by putting on the belt of truth! That is the way you overcome and walk victoriously in this life!

Prayer: *Lord, I am so grateful for this salvation! It is so amazing! It is called the great salvation. Lord, it is marvelous that You would love me so much You want to be near me. You put Your very self inside me. Father, please help me to grasp this truth. Help me to wrap this truth around my very core and not allow this wondrous truth to be something that is merely head knowledge but, instead, is in my heart and the place of Your dwelling. In Jesus' Name!*

STUDY QUESTIONS

> Be diligent to present yourself approved to God, a worker
> who does not need to be ashamed, rightly dividing the word of truth.
> — 2 Timothy 2:15

1. In your own words, explain Ephesians 6:12. And in Ephesians 6:13, what is the spiritual defense we have been provided by God?

2. According to First Peter 1:18 and 19, how were you bought out of slavery? What does this mean to your daily walk with the Lord?

3. Describe the function of the "buckler" during times of war in Paul's day. What does having Christ as your Buckler mean for you today?

PRACTICAL APPLICATION

> But be doers of the word,
> and not hearers only, deceiving yourselves.
> — James 1:22

Cultivate commitment as you run your race.

1. Explain an instance in your walk with the Lord when a Scripture that was head knowledge became heart knowledge. How did it happen?

2. In what area of your life have you had to deal with the enemy? How did you overcome his accusations to become free?

3. How does knowing that your life is not your own bring freedom?

LESSON 2

TOPIC

Righteousness Is Your Breastplate

SCRIPTURES

1. **Ephesians 6:13,14** — Therefore take up the whole armor of God, that you may be able to withstand in the evil day, and having done all, to stand. Stand therefore, having girded your waist with truth, having put on the breastplate of righteousness.

2. **2 Timothy 4:3,4** — For the time will come when they will not endure sound doctrine, but according to their own desires, because they have itching ears, they heap up for themselves teachers; and they will turn their ears away from the truth, and be turned aside to fables.

3. **John 16:8** — And when He has come, He will convict the world of sin, and of righteousness, and of judgment.

4. **Romans 3:21-26** — But now the righteousness of God apart from the law is revealed, being witnessed by the Law and the Prophets, even the

righteousness of God, through faith in Jesus Christ, to all and on all who believe. For there is no difference; for all have sinned and fall short of the glory of God, being justified freely by His grace through the redemption that is in Christ Jesus, whom God set forth as a propitiation by His blood, through faith, to demonstrate His righteousness, because in His forbearance God had passed over the sins that were previously committed, to demonstrate at the present time His righteousness, that He might be just and the justifier of the one who has faith in Jesus.

5. **2 Corinthians 5:21** — For He made Him who knew no sin to be sin for us, that we might become the righteousness of God in Him.

6. **Romans 8:1** — There is therefore now no condemnation to those who are in Christ Jesus, who do not walk according to the flesh, but according to the Spirit.

SYNOPSIS

The armor of God, as described in Ephesians 6:11-18, is essential to our ability to live successfully as children of God in this world. The belt of truth, which is the Word of God, is vital to a victorious life on this earth. And the breastplate of righteousness, the next weapon in God's armor, is necessary for battling against the schemes the enemy plots against us.

The emphasis of this lesson:

Without knowledge of or accessing the breastplate of righteousness, we will be confronted with repeated accusations from the enemy, often resulting in condemnation. When we get a revelation of the fact that we have been made the righteousness of God in Christ Jesus, we will walk free in our mind and soul from the lies that have kept us bound.

Lawlessness

We are living in the last-of-the-last days. What is good is being called evil and what is evil, good. Lying has become commonplace, and the world is being increasingly drawn to evil and lawlessness. The Bible warned us of these things. Second Timothy 4:3 and 4 states, "For the time will come when they will not endure sound doctrine, but according to their own desires, because they have itching ears, they heap up for themselves teachers; and they will turn their ears away from the truth, and be turned aside to fables." But lawlessness must occur before the man of lawlessness appears. And although lawlessness is rampant in the day in which we are living, as born-again believers, we do not need to be afraid. We have been given amazing equipment and armor to stand against the enemy!

Truth Dissipates Lies

As we saw in Lesson 1, the first weapon in our arsenal against the enemy is the belt of truth, which is the Word of God. God's Word will enable us to stand firm against every lie of the enemy. One of his tactics is to gain access into your mind, and one of the ways he does this is by speaking lies or statements that are counter to the Word of God. For example, the Bible tells us we are more than conquerors. But the enemy whispers, "Look at your checkbook. It's in the red, and you think *you* are more than a conqueror? If things don't change, you'll be filing for bankruptcy and soon be out on the street and homeless!"

The enemy will do anything he can to plant lies in our thoughts to turn our focus away from God's promises and who He made us to be in Christ Jesus. That's the reason it is so important to wrap the first piece of the armor of God — the belt of truth — tightly around our waist. Truth will dissipate every lie of the enemy and cause us to become victorious against him!

A Revelation of Righteousness

The next weapon of our spiritual armor is the breastplate of righteousness. And in her program, Denise shared a personal story about this particular weapon.

> When I was in college, I loved the Lord with all my heart and served Him the best I was able to at the time. But I had a constant cloud of condemnation that seemed to hang over me. I knew I was a Christian, but I truly believed that I was the worst believer on the face of the planet.
>
> Negative thoughts would speak loudly, *You're not enough. You just don't measure up. God is not pleased with you. Yes, He may love you, but He does not take pleasure in you.* These thoughts were relentless, and because I believed them at the time, they resulted in depression and hopelessness. If I was praying, serving God in some manner, witnessing, or leading someone to the Lord, I felt okay about myself. But if I wasn't actively participating in something I

thought was pleasing to the Lord, I would allow condemnation to flood my soul.

Sometimes I would speak to my college roommate about it and say things like, "I am so depressed. I really don't know why." And she would respond, "Denise, that's ridiculous! You love God, and you are precious to Him."

One day I was listening to a message by Kenneth E. Hagin. He was teaching about God's righteousness. Even while I listened to that message, I was still arguing within myself that I was not righteous. I actually listened to that message two times when I heard the Lord say, "Who are you going to believe — yourself, your mind, or My Word?" When the Holy Spirit spoke that to me, it stopped me right where I was and I prayed, "Lord, I need to believe You." On that very day, I received a revelation and accepted my righteousness through Christ Jesus!

John 16:8-10 says, "And when He has come, He will convict the world of sin, and of righteousness, and of judgment: of sin, because they do not believe in Me; of righteousness, because I go to My Father and you see Me no more." When I saw this passage, I realized that just saying, "I'm righteous" or deciding to act righteous did not make me righteous. The only way to receive and understand God's righteousness is by the conviction and revelation of the Holy Spirit. Before this revelation was imparted to me by the Holy Spirit, I did not believe I was accepted by God or that I was righteous in His sight. But once the Holy Spirit imparted this truth, I have never been the same!

The breastplate of righteousness intimidates the devil. He does not want us to know that we are the righteousness of God in Christ Jesus. When we understand this truth, it instills confidence and courage within us to overcome every lie the enemy hurls our way.

He Became Sin So We Could Become Righteous

Romans 3:21 and 22 states, "But now the righteousness of God apart from the law is revealed, being witnessed by the Law and the Prophets, even the righteousness of God, through faith in Jesus Christ, to all and on all who believe. For there is no difference." The righteousness of God only comes to us through our faith in Jesus Christ. It does not come to us because we do good works, tithe, fast, witness, or forgive someone. The righteousness of God only comes by faith — and even that faith originates with God!

Romans 3:23-26 continues, "For all have sinned and fall short of the glory of God, being justified freely by His grace through the redemption that is in Christ Jesus, whom God set forth as a propitiation by His blood, through faith, to demonstrate His righteousness, because in His forbearance God had passed over the sins that were previously committed, to demonstrate at the present time His righteousness, that He might be just and the justifier of the one who has faith in Jesus."

Verse 23 highlights the fact that *every* believer born on this earth has missed the glory of God He wants us to have. We *all* have sinned and fallen short of His glory, but God passed over the sins that we previously committed to demonstrate His righteousness.

On the program, Denise said, "I am not perfect, and neither are you. My mind is not perfect, my emotions are not perfect, and my body is not perfect. But the moment I accepted Jesus as my Lord and Savior and received the revelation that I am the righteousness of God in Christ Jesus, I could walk free of guilt and condemnation! So often as believers we can get caught up in good works and we start thinking it is all about us, but it's *not* about us. It is about what He did, and there is so much freedom that comes when we simply say, 'Lord, it is not about me, it is about what You did on my behalf. I am so grateful for the Cross, and I am the righteousness of God in Christ Jesus!'"

It was God's idea to choose us, cleanse us, and deliver us. It was His idea to live inside of us and make our body the temple of the Holy Spirit.

Jesus, who is absolutely sinless, was made sin for us to destroy the sin we were born into at birth and make available to us God's righteousness through being born-again. Second Corinthians 5:21 states, "For He made Him who knew no sin to be sin for us, that we might become the righteousness of God in Him."

The instant we accepted Jesus as our Savior, we were completely accepted in the Beloved, made the righteousness of God in our spirit, and given the breastplate of righteousness as part of our spiritual armor. We put on that breastplate by acknowledging we are the temple of God. He dwells in us, and we are the very righteousness of God. When the devil sees that breastplate of righteousness, it absolutely intimidates him. You have the Greater One dwelling on the inside of you! And that is Good News!

Prayer: *Father, I want to thank You for these amazing weapons You have given us to fight the enemy. The belt of truth and the breastplate of righteousness provide us with the weapons we need to dispel every lie and accusation of the enemy against our soul. We glorify You, Lord, for Your greatness, Your grace, and Your mercy towards us every day. Help us to recognize the amazing armor You have provided us with that is available inside our spirit and will never be taken away. We give you all the praise! In the precious, magnificent, and wonderful name of Jesus!*

STUDY QUESTIONS

Be diligent to present yourself approved to God, a worker
who does not need to be ashamed, rightly dividing the word of truth.
— 2 Timothy 2:15

1. According to Matthew 24:12 and Second Timothy 4:4, what are some of the consequences of lawlessness?
2. What are the "wiles" of the devil (*see* Ephesians 6:11), and how do we stand against them?
3. How does true righteousness come to us from God? (*See* Romans 3:22.)
4. Describe what "righteousness apart from the law" means according to Romans 3:21-23.

PRACTICAL APPLICATION

But be doers of the word,
and not hearers only, deceiving yourselves.
— James 1:22

Learn to listen to God's details.

1. Describe a time when you experienced an extended time of condemnation in your life. What verse or verses did you use to overcome?
2. How has your understanding of the righteousness of God helped you stand against the accusations of the enemy?

3. How does understanding that you are the righteousness of God in Christ change your perspective on how you view yourself?

4. Name one instance where you have overcome a repeated lie of the enemy after understanding you have been made the righteousness of God in Christ Jesus.

TOPIC

Walk in Shoes of Peace

SCRIPTURES

1. **Ephesians 6:15** — And having shod your feet with the preparation of the gospel of peace.

2. **Mark 4:38** — But He was in the stern, asleep on a pillow. And they awoke Him and said to Him, "Teacher, do You not care that we are perishing?"

3. **John 20:19,21,26** — Then, the same day at evening, being the first day of the week, when the doors were shut where the disciples were assembled, for fear of the Jews, Jesus came and stood in the midst, and said to them, "Peace be with you."…So Jesus said to them again, "Peace to you! As the Father has sent Me, I also send you."…And after eight days His disciples were again inside, and Thomas with them. Jesus came, the doors being shut, and stood in the midst, and said, "Peace to you."

4. **Philippians 4:7** — …and the peace of God, which surpasses all understanding, will guard your hearts and minds through Christ Jesus.

SYNOPSIS

Another important aspect of the armor of God is the shoes we wear. To stand strong against the enemy we must put on the shoes of peace. But peace does not mean passivity. God's peace is aggressive because it threatens the success of the attacks of the enemy and conquers his chaos and confusion. It is a peace that confounds the human mind because its source is found in God.

The emphasis of this lesson:

Jesus is called the "Prince of Peace." He told His disciples, "Peace I leave with you, My peace I give to you; not as the world gives do I give to you…" (John 14:27). His peace is a supernatural peace that passes human understanding (*see* Philippians 4:7), and it's one of our greatest weapons against the attacks of the enemy.

Peace Shoes

We have been given spiritual armor to protect us from the works, power, and attacks of the devil. The Bible says we are not fighting against flesh and blood, which are things in the natural. Our fight is against "principalities, against powers, against the rulers of the darkness of this age, [and] against spiritual hosts of wickedness in the heavenly places" (Ephesians 6:12). The devil believes he is very powerful, but he is not more powerful than the One who dwells inside your born-again spirit. If you could see yourself in the spirit, you would see that you have been clothed in the armor of God.

In the first two lessons, we expounded upon the belt of truth, which is the Word of God, and the breastplate of righteousness. Both are powerful weapons against the slanderous accusations of the enemy. Another essential part of the armor we have been given is found in Ephesians 6:15, which says, "And having shod your feet with the preparation of the gospel of peace." The shoes of peace are powerful to walk over, stomp on, and crush the attacks of the devil. Many imagine peace to be passive. However, God's peace is a conquering peace, and it is aggressive and threatening toward all the works of the enemy.

Peace in the Storm

Jesus displayed God's peace in His life while He was on this earth. The gospel of Mark recounts a time when Jesus stepped into a boat and pushed away from the shore so He could more effectively teach the multitude that had gathered around Him. As He sat on the boat, He shared many parables.

When evening arrived, Jesus said to His disciples, "Let us cross over to the other side" (Mark 4:35). But while they were crossing over the sea, they encountered a great windstorm, probably similar to a cyclone. The disciples could feel and hear the wind, as the waves of water filled the boat. The storm was completely engulfing them, and they were probably wondering if they would ever see their loved ones again.

Fear began to fill them and drown any hope of surviving. They were probably yelling, "Do something, Peter! Do something, Luke! Do something, John!" But while the disciples panicked, Jesus slept in perfect peace. Verse 38 says, "But He was in the stern, asleep on a pillow. And they awoke Him and said to Him, "Teacher, do You not care that we are perishing?"

Mark 4:39 describes what happened next. "Then He arose and rebuked the wind, and said to the sea, 'Peace be still!' And the wind ceased the there was a great calm." From a place of peace, Jesus *rebuked* the wind and *spoke* to the sea, and both had to obey His command.

The Power of Peace

On the program, Denise recounted a story that a woman had shared with her about the power of God's peace.

> This woman lived in an apartment complex and the walls were very thin. Every night, her next-door neighbors played loud music. At a time of night when most people were sleeping, her neighbors were yelling loudly and blaring their music. The woman complained, but nothing was ever done to stop it.

> This went on night after night, and she was losing precious sleep. Then she came across my teaching on peace and how Jesus was able to sleep during the storm, and she declared, "I've got that same peace!" And for the first time in a very long time, she was filled with God's peace and slept through the night! Peace is a powerful weapon we have been given.

When Jesus' empty tomb was discovered, the disciples were afraid for their lives, so they gathered together in a private room and locked the door. John 20:19 states, "Then, the same day at evening, being the first day of the week, when the doors were shut where the disciples were assembled, for fear of the Jews, Jesus came and stood in the midst, and said to them, '*Peace* be with you.'" Their Friend and Savior, whom they had just buried, was now standing before them. And Jesus' first word to them was "peace."

The disciples were put at ease and then glad to see the Lord. And, again, Jesus said to them, "*Peace* to you!" (John 20:21) "And after eight days His disciples were again inside, and Thomas with them. Jesus came, the doors being shut, and stood in the midst, and said, '*Peace* to you!'" (John 20:26)

Jesus had to repeatedly speak peace to the disciples because they were consumed with fear. They had committed their lives to Jesus and had followed Him continuously for three years. They had eaten with Him, laughed with Him, and rested and slept where He rested and slept. They had watched Him perform miracles over and over again.

But then the disciples watched as the Romans crucified Jesus. They watched as He died on the Cross, and they watched as Jesus' body was placed in the tomb. They were very afraid because they felt uncertain about their future. But each time Jesus appeared to them, He spoke *peace*. God's peace has the power to shatter and destroy every doubt and fear that could ever plague our heart.

We are living in troubling times, but we can walk in peace because Jesus Christ IS Perfect Peace, and He dwells inside us. Peace is an essential weapon in our spiritual armor. We can stand — and stand firm — because of the peace that has been placed upon our feet. Wherever we go, His peace goes with us. God's peace also has a voice — it will say *no* to fear and *no* to worry. Paul was in prison when he wrote Ephesians; the Holy Spirit opened his eyes to the spiritual armor on the inside, including the shoes of peace.

Philippians 4:7 declares, "And the peace of God, which surpasses all understanding, will guard your hearts and minds through Christ Jesus." God's peace bypasses our human understanding. We can be surrounded by chaos and storms can be raging around us, yet we can be filled with a supernatural peace that only comes from God.

Killer Shoes

In Romans 16:20, Paul exhorted the believers when he said, "…The God of peace will crush Satan under your feet shortly.…" The word "crush" in Greek means *to bring to nothing* or *to crush as into powder*. God's shoes of peace have the power to crush, annihilate, and make as nothing. Every attack of the enemy is under your feet, which are shod with the gospel of peace! So you, with your feet secure in His peace, have the power to crush the enemy!

As Roman soldiers walked the streets in early New Testament times, they displayed great strength and athletic aptitude — and they wore killer shoes. These were not typical sandals worn by the common people of that day. The shoes worn by Roman soldiers had spikes on the bottom of the shoes that were one to two inches long. As they walked through the towns and villages, anything under their feet would be crushed beneath them and left as if it had never existed!

This is the picture Paul used to describe the spiritual shoes of peace that are upon our feet. When the devil comes to steal our peace, our joy, or our patience, we can walk right over those attacks, and leave them as dust under our feet. We can crush every assault with the powerful killer shoes of peace. God did not leave us powerless, but instead, He filled us full of His power, which enables us to stand against any enemy and crush them under our feet with these killer shoes!

When we agree with the Word that says we have the Prince of Peace on the inside and our feet have been shod with the gospel of peace, we can crush every enemy that comes against us!

Prayer: *Lord, we receive Your peace, which is part of our spiritual armor. We speak peace to the storms in our bodies, in our relationships, and in our finances, and we acknowledge the killer shoes of peace You have given us to crush every attack that comes against us! In the mighty name of Jesus! Amen!*

STUDY QUESTIONS

Be diligent to present yourself approved to God, a worker
who does not need to be ashamed, rightly dividing the word of truth.
— 2 Timothy 2:15

1. When Jesus arose from the dead, why were the disciples so filled with fear? How did Jesus address those fears?
2. Describe the shoes that the Roman soldiers wore as part of their armor. What was most significant about them and how does that translate to the spiritual armor given to us by God?

PRACTICAL APPLICATION

But be doers of the word,
and not hearers only, deceiving yourselves.
—James 1:22

Learn to run your race with forgiveness and wisdom!

1. Describe a time in your life when you struggled with a lack of peace. Write down one verse that the Lord ministered to you during that time and how it transformed your thinking.

2. All believers have faced storms in life. Think about a time when a storm was raging around you and how you allowed God's peace to conquer it.

TOPIC

Take Up the Shield of Faith

SCRIPTURES

1. **Ephesians 4:24** — And that you put on the new man which was created according to God, in true righteousness and holiness.

2. **Ephesians 6:16** — Above all, taking the shield of faith with which you will be able to quench all the fiery darts of the wicked one.

3. **2 Kings 4:30** — And the mother of the child said, "As the Lord lives, and as your soul lives, I will not leave you." So he arose and followed her.

SYNOPSIS

The shield of faith is another essential piece of the armor of God that can ensure a victorious life in Christ. The Roman soldier's shield, which is referred to in Ephesians 6:16, covered the Roman soldier from head to toe. It had tremendous protective power and instilled confidence in the soldier who bore it. With the shield of faith in operation, we can quench every fiery attack of the enemy that confronts us in our daily lives.

The emphasis of this lesson:

The story of the Shunammite woman in Second Kings 4 is a powerful example of someone wielding their shield of faith. When her only son died suddenly, she only spoke words of faith as she sought help from Elisha the prophet. The Shunammite woman activated her shield of faith through the words she spoke, and her son lived. Her unwavering faith continues to serve as an example for us today!

A Quick Review of Our Spiritual Weapons

In Ephesians, the apostle Paul let us know that we have not been left defenseless against the strategies of the enemy. And these lessons have been a great reminder of the power we have at our disposal, not only to defend ourselves against the devil, but the God-given spiritual weapons we have to put *him* on the run!

First, we saw the importance of the belt of truth — the written Word of God — which is the most important piece of weaponry that we possess. If we keep His Word before our eyes, it equips us to battle against the lies and accusations of the devil.

Then we focused on the breastplate of righteousness. We cannot create this righteousness on our own, nor can we understand it without the revelation of the Holy Spirit. But we are, in fact, the very righteousness of God in Christ Jesus! We cannot work for it or earn it — it is a free gift from God. But without embracing this part of our spiritual armor, the enemy can keep us bound with his lies, accusations, and condemnation. As we acknowledge we are the righteousness of God, we are putting that breastplate of righteousness into action.

We also studied the shoes of peace — killer shoes placed upon our feet to crush, annihilate, and demolish the work of the devil. Whenever he tries to bring situations and accusations against us, we simply acknowledge the powerful shoes we are wearing, given to us by the Prince of Peace!

The next piece of spiritual armor we'll unpack is the shield of faith. Ephesians 6:16 says, "Above all, taking the shield of faith with which you will be able to quench all the fiery darts of the wicked one." When confronting a Roman soldier, the first thing an enemy saw was the warrior's shield. It was out in front of the warrior and protected him from the flaming arrows the enemy was sending his way. The enemy also sees *our* shield of faith if it is activated in our lives. God's faithfulness goes before us and can move past anything currently happening in our lives.

The Shield of Faith and the Shunammite Woman

There is an amazing story in the Old Testament of a woman who used her shield of faith to save the life of her son. Although the woman's name is never mentioned, she is described in the Bible as "the Shunammite woman" (*see* 2 Kings 4:8-37). This woman loved and honored the prophet

Elisha. Every time he was traveling by her house, she would prepare him a meal.

In the days of the Old Testament, it was the prophets who spoke for the Lord. The Shunammite woman hungered for more of God, so she asked her husband to build a room for Elisha to stay in whenever he was traveling through their town. In appreciation for the woman's generosity, Elisha asked his servant what they might be able to do for her. His servant responded, "…She has no son, and her husband is old" (2 Kings 4:14). Elisha sent for her and prophesied, "Next year you will have a son" (see v. 16), and it happened as Elisha had spoken.

As the Shunammite woman's son grew, he helped his father in the fields. But one day the boy suddenly cried out, "My head hurts!" The boy was carried to his mother, but as she held him in her lap, he died. Without speaking a negative word, the woman laid the boy on the bed Elisha slept on when he was in town. She then sent a message to her husband asking him to send her a servant and a donkey so she could travel to see Elisha.

When her husband questioned her request, she simply responded, "It is well" (see v. 23). She saddled the donkey and she and the servant hurried to Elisha's home in Mount Carmel. As they approached Elisha's home, he saw her and sent his servant to run and greet her and to ask her if everything was alright with her husband and child. Again she answered, "It is well" (see v. 26).

When she was face-to-face with Elisha, she fell at his feet. Elisha knew her soul was in deep distress. The Shunammite woman said to Elisha, "Did I ask a son of my lord? Did I not say, 'Do not deceive me?'" (2 Kings 4:28). So Elisha sent his servant with Elisha's staff to lay on the child's face, but the Shunammite woman insisted that Elisha accompany her home, and he did.

The Bible then tells us, "When Elisha came into the house, there was the child, lying dead on his bed. He went in therefore, shut the door behind the two of them, and prayed to the Lord. And he went up and lay on the child, and put his mouth on his mouth, his eyes on his eyes, and his hands on his hands; and he stretched himself out on the child, and the flesh of the child became warm. He returned and walked back and forth in the house, and again went up and stretched himself out on him; then the child sneezed seven times, and the child opened his eyes. And he called Gehazi and said, 'Call this Shunammite woman.' So he called her. And when she came in to him, he said, 'Pick up your son.' So she went in, fell at his feet, and bowed to the ground; then she picked up her son and went out" (2 Kings 4:32-37).

Each time the Shunammite woman was questioned along her journey, she spoke "It is well." Despite the natural circumstances and deep distress of her soul, the woman lifted her shield of faith. She knew the prophet had promised her this son and that God had supernaturally blessed the fruit of her once-barren womb. She knew that God did not deliver this promise only for her son to be taken from her prematurely. She kept her focus on the God who delivers, lifted her shield of faith, and spoke, "It is well."

Lifting Up the Shield of Faith

On the program, Denise shared a personal story.

> Many years ago, Rick and I had a friend, James, who was a famous bodybuilder. One day he was in a horrible car accident. His entire body was covered with bandages and casts. His neck was wrapped with a brace and the doctors told him he would never walk again. They told him he would have difficulty moving his arms and would be a paraplegic for the rest of his life.
>
> But James' wife said to him, 'Sweetheart, you know the Word of God. You know that by the stripes of Jesus, you were healed. You must take hold of the power of God.' James received that encouragement from his wife. And even though he was confronted with tremendous pain, his body was broken, and the doctors continued to say he would never walk again, he began to speak over his body, 'It is well.' He lifted up that shield of faith and quenched every fiery dart of the wicked one by the words he spoke.
>
> Today James is completely healed! He is walking and serving in church, and you would never know he had ever been in such a severe accident.

Denise also shared the testimony of a woman who was diagnosed with multiple sclerosis. She had lost sight in one eye and the feeling on one side of her body. Everyone was planning her funeral and telling her she needed to give up. They were saying she had false hope.

But this woman decided to raise her shield of faith and speak life to her situation. She said, "It is well with me. I am going to raise my children, play tennis with my kids, and live a long life with my husband and the family God has given me." This woman began to imagine herself playing with her children and traveling with her husband. She filled her heart with the Word of God and only allowed God's Word to fill her house. She did not give up. She lifted her shield of faith, and she was healed! She regained her eyesight, and the feeling and movement were restored to her body.

When you were born again, the very faith of God was given to you, and you believed what you could not see with your physical eyes. You could not *see* the faith to be saved, and you could not *see* the love of God. You could not *see* the blood of Jesus cleansing you from all unrighteousness.

Likewise, we have been given the shield of faith, and even though we cannot see it with our physical eyes, we need to activate it in our lives. We need to put the shield of faith out in front of us and say, "Devil, I am moving forward. I am not listening to your lies. I am not receiving your intimidation, and I am moving forward."

Like the Shunammite woman, we must choose to speak, "It is well." We are not powerless. We have God-given faith on the inside to push through any obstacle. We are not victims; we are victors! We are not the conquered; we are conquerors through the faith God has imparted to us!

Prayer: *Father, You are so magnificent. Thank You for Your grace and mercy poured out on us and for the faith You have freely given us. This faith is so powerful that it quenches all the fiery darts of the wicked one. Lord, we give You praise. We believe Your Word and lift our shield of faith. We give you all the praise and the glory. In Jesus' name!*

STUDY QUESTIONS

> Be diligent to present yourself approved to God, a worker
> who does not need to be ashamed, rightly dividing the word of truth.
> — 2 Timothy 2:15

1. Compare the story of the Shunammite woman found in Second Kings 4 to Mary, the mother of Jesus, when she received the words spoken to her by the angel. What was Mary's shield of faith?
2. Ephesians 6:17 describes two more weapons of the armor of God. What are they and how do they protect you?

3. How is the kind of prayer found in Ephesians 6:18 connected to successfully utilizing the armor of God in the life of the believer?

PRACTICAL APPLICATION

**But be doers of the word,
and not hearers only, deceiving yourselves.
— James 1:22**

Don't let the enemy push you out of your race!

1. How are you currently using the shield of faith in your life? What words are you speaking despite your circumstances to activate the shield of faith?

2. If negative circumstances have been dominating your life, describe how you plan to use the armor of God to overcome them.

3. Do you have a testimony about a time you raised your shield of faith to overcome a difficult circumstance? What words did you speak and what actions did you take to overcome the situation?

LESSON 5

TOPIC

The Power of Your Helmet, Your Sword, and Your Prayers

SCRIPTURES

1. **Ephesians 6:12-18** — For we do not wrestle against flesh and blood, but against principalities, against powers, against the rulers of the darkness of this age, against spiritual hosts of wickedness in the heavenly places. Therefore take up the whole armor of God, that you may be able to withstand in the evil day, and having done all, to stand. Stand therefore, having girded your waist with truth, having put on the breastplate of righteousness, and having shod your feet with the preparation of the gospel of peace; above all, taking the shield of faith with which you will be able to quench all the fiery darts of the wicked one. And take the helmet of salvation, and the sword of the Spirit,

which is the word of God; praying always with all prayer and supplication in the Spirit, being watchful to this end with all perseverance and supplication for all the saints.

2. **1 Peter 1:18** — Knowing that you were not redeemed with corruptible things, like silver or gold, from your aimless conduct received by tradition from your fathers.

3. **2 Corinthians 5:17** — Therefore, if anyone is in Christ, he is a new creation; old things have passed away; behold, all things have become new.

4. **Isaiah 54:2** — Enlarge the place of your tent, and let them stretch out the curtains of your dwellings; Do not spare; Lengthen your cords, and strengthen your stakes.

SYNOPSIS

Ephesians 6:12-18 is an important passage for every believer because it describes the spiritual weapons that are available to all who will learn to access and wield them. He has given us the Holy Spirit and has fashioned for us a spiritual armor that can defeat the principalities, powers, rulers of the darkness of this age, and the spiritual hosts of wickedness in the heavenly places. No, God has not left us as orphans nor powerless on this earth. He has supernaturally equipped us to live an overcoming life!

The emphasis of this lesson:

At the point of our salvation, a helmet was placed upon our head to protect us from attacks upon our minds and thoughts. Combined with renewing our minds with God's Word, we cannot be defeated. The Word of God, which is the sword of the Spirit, has the power to defeat any weapons the enemy has formed against us.

The Amazing Armor of God

We have been studying the armor of God as described by Paul in Ephesians. Paul exhorts us to put on the whole armor of God and reminds us of who it is that we are standing against. Ephesians 6:13-18 says, "Therefore take up the whole armor of God, that you may be able to withstand in the evil day, and having done all, to stand. Stand therefore, having girded your waist with truth, having put on the breastplate of righteousness, and having shod your feet with the preparation of the gospel of peace; above all, taking the shield of faith with which you will be able to quench all the fiery darts of the wicked one. And take the helmet of salvation, and the sword of the Spirit, which is the word of God; praying always with all prayer and supplication in the Spirit, being watchful to this end with all perseverance and supplication for all the saints."

God has not left us powerless or as orphans in this world. An orphan has no family to protect him or her, little or no financial support, and is typically someone in need of help. Jesus promised, "I will not leave you orphans" (John 14:18). Through Jesus' finished work on the Cross, we have been grafted into the family of God and are loved with an immeasurable love. The Holy Spirit came to live in us, and we have been clothed with the armor of God. No, we are not orphans, and we are not powerless.

When the Holy Spirit came to live inside us, the armor of God was also deposited within us. But to be able to operate in the power these spiritual weapons provide, we need to know what they are and what they are used for. The apostle Paul let us know that our fight is not against flesh and blood, but against principalities, powers, rulers of the darkness of this age, and evil spirits in the heavenly place (*see* Ephesians 6:12). So to effectively use our God-given weapons, we must remember who the real enemy is.

In Lesson 1, we examined the belt of truth — God's Word. The Word of God is the most important part of our spiritual armor. When we get the written Word of God into our heart, it can change the way we think. If we are dealing with sickness or disease or relational issues, the Word can open our eyes to the fact that we don't need to put up with these issues in our life. We have power through Jesus Christ!

When we were born again, God redeemed us and came to live inside us. We were bought with a price. First Peter 1:18 and 19 says, "Knowing that you were not redeemed with corruptible things, like silver or gold, from your aimless conduct received by tradition from your fathers, but with the precious blood of Christ, as of a lamb without blemish and without spot." Jesus was the perfect sacrificial lamb, and He paid the price for our sin.

Another piece of our spiritual armor is the breastplate of righteousness. Second Corinthians 5:21 declares, "For He made Him who knew no sin to be sin for us, that we might become the righteousness of God in Him." We are not righteous from right doing, but we are counted as righteous because God placed within us *His* righteousness through faith in Jesus Christ. Try as we might, we can never be good enough on our own to be righteous before God, but because of the finished work of the Cross, Jesus' righteousness has made us righteous.

Next, we unpacked the shoes of peace. But these shoes are also aggressive shoes and mighty against the assaults of the enemy. When the devil tries to bring chaos or disturbance to steal our joy or tempt us with thoughts of confusion, we can simply say *no* to the strategies of the enemy and choose to abide in the peace of God that belongs to us. This God-given peace is one of the great weapons against the enemy.

We also studied the shield of faith. It's the first thing the enemy sees when he comes against us. First John 5:4 says, "For whatever is born of God overcomes the world. And this is the victory that has overcome the world — our faith." This is the faith we were freely given at the time of our salvation — God gave us faith to believe on Him. And faith is strengthened by spending time in the Word of God. When we draw upon that faith, it will quench and stop the fiery darts of the wicked one.

The Helmet of Salvation

The list of our spiritual armor continues in Ephesians 6:17, which says, "And take the helmet of salvation…." The helmet worn by a Roman soldier in Early New Testament times was typically made of bronze, and it was extremely heavy. Fortunately for the soldier, the inside of the helmet was filled with a spongy material to soften the weight of it on the soldier's head. This piece of armor protected the soldier's head and prevented the enemy armies from knocking him out or beheading him.

As the apostle Paul observed the importance of the helmet to a Roman soldier, he began to liken it to the power of our salvation. Our salvation is the greatest gift that God has ever given us. The moment we are saved, the helmet of salvation is placed upon our head to protect our minds and thoughts from the onslaught of lies and accusations from the enemy.

When the devil comes to attack, he first tries to penetrate the mind. But when we spend time in the Word of God and strengthen our mind with His thoughts toward us — what God says about our salvation, redemption, healing, and so much more — it shields us from the lies of the enemy. The devil can not get past our impenetrable helmet of salvation!

The Sword of the Spirit

In addition to the helmet of salvation, we have also been given the sword of the Spirit, which is the *spoken* Word of God. Ephesians 6:17 continues, "And take the helmet of salvation, and the sword of the Spirit, which is the word of God. The Greek word for "word" is *rhema*, which refers to a specific revealed word illuminated by the Holy Spirit and *spoken* by the recipient of the revelation.

On the program, Denise shared the following story:

> Many years ago, my husband spent a lot of time traveling and teaching. He was often gone for two or three weeks, and I was home alone with the boys. Every time Rick was able to be home, I found myself upset with him. I didn't understand my emotions or my actions at the time. The longer he was able to be home, it seemed I would become less upset, but the minute I had to drive him to the airport for another trip, I would find myself being very upset with him again.
>
> I would cry while driving Rick to the airport because he was leaving again. And I would think, *I didn't marry you just to be separated all the time. I married you to be with you. I don't like being alone or raising the boys by myself.* My attitude, anger, and emotions, even when Rick was home, were very negative. I didn't know why I was so angry.
>
> One day I prayed and said, "Lord, You have got to help me do something about this. My attitude is not pleasant for Rick, and I cannot continue crying constantly each time I drive him to or from the airport." I was allowing the devil to steal my peace, cause discomfort and contention in my home, and paint a negative picture of the family for my sons.
>
> When I cried out for help, the Holy Spirit opened my eyes to Isaiah 54:2, which says, "Enlarge the place of your tent, and let them stretch out the curtains of your dwellings; Do not spare; Lengthen your cords, and strengthen your stakes."
>
> As I read that verse, the Holy Spirit said, "Denise, you have a choice. You can either enlarge the place of your tent by enlarging your heart to receive what is happening with your husband,

opening your heart to receive from Me, having an attitude of pride and joy for your husband, and supporting him, or you can have this set of emotions filled with resentment, depression, sadness, confusion and not paint the right picture for your boys. Denise, you choose. You can stretch forth and receive what I have for you, or you can stay in this old attitude."

That was a "sword of the Spirit" moment for me in my life. I did not do it perfectly, but I determined that I would turn away from those wrong attitudes and emotions and speak God's Word over Rick, our marriage, our family, and our ministry. I chose to be proud, happy, and supportive of my husband. Like a sword, that one word from God was thrust into the enemy and removed his power to disturb me, to disturb our boys, and to disturb our marriage. That's how powerful one word from God is to destroy the enemy.

The Road and a Rhema Word

Denise shared another story concerning the Word of God on the program:

There was another time earlier in our lives when God called us to take our ministry on the road. We had been pastors and were part of a local body of believers. We were somewhat comfortable about where we were, but then God spoke to Rick, "I want you to go on the road and preach the Gospel to any church that will open its doors."

At the time, Paul was two years old, and I was pregnant with Philip. When I married Rick, I committed to follow him as he followed God. When he told me God had called him to go on the road, fear came to me. I began to question the Lord, *What are we going to do? How are we going to take care of Paul and the new baby that is on its way? How are we going to live? Lord, I need to hear from You!*

One morning while I was worshiping the Lord, the answer to my questions came. I looked down at my feet and a rhema word from the Holy Spirit came to me. The Lord said to me, "I do direct the steps of a righteous man." I responded, "Okay, Lord. You are directing Rick's steps, and therefore, You are directing *our* steps, and we are going to be okay."

The enemy tries to bring worry, care, and fear. But when the word of the Lord rises up in your spirit, comes into your heart, and out of your mouth, it completely severs the plans, schemes, and lies of the devil! The sword of the Spirit — the spoken word of God — is a powerful weapon we have been given from God!

Intimacy In Prayer

Our relationship with God began with our mouth. We believed in our heart that Jesus is Lord and that God raised Him from the dead and we *confessed it with our mouth*. Prayer is our communication with Him. God delights in us when we talk to Him, but He also wants to talk to us. There is no more intimate relationship in our lives than our communication with God through prayer and worship.

First Corinthians 6:17 says, "But he who is joined to the Lord is one spirit with Him." When we pray, *Lord, I don't know what to do about this situation, but I'm inviting the Holy Spirit to help me*, or when we speak against sickness in the authority and power of the name of Jesus, it is all prayer, and prayer contains the power to stop the enemy in his attacks against us. You don't need to feel helpless or afraid because of everything that's going on in the world. He has placed within you the armor necessary to defeat every scheme, lie, and attack of the enemy!

First John 4:4 reminds us, "You are of God, little children and have overcome them, because He who is in you is greater than he who is in the world." The Greater One lives inside us, and He is greater than any fear, greater than any sickness, greater than any relational problem, greater than any confusion or doubt, and greater than anything we will ever face in this life. And we have His Word on that!

Prayer: *Father, we thank You and praise You for Your presence in our lives. You said our body is the temple of the Holy Spirit. Please help us to recognize and align ourselves with the great power that dwells inside us by the Holy Spirit. Thank you for access to the powerful weapons you have placed inside us including the belt of truth, the breastplate of righteousness, the shoes of peace, the shield of faith, the helmet of salvation, the sword of the Spirit, and the power of prayer. Lord, we thank you for it all and acknowledge the power available to us. In Jesus' name! Amen!*

STUDY QUESTIONS

Be diligent to present yourself approved to God, a worker
who does not need to be ashamed, rightly dividing the word of truth.
— 2 Timothy 2:15

1. List the spiritual weapons described in Ephesians 6:12-18.
    Describe a weapon you have used most recently. What was the result?
2. What is prayer? Why is it important to the life of a born-again
    believer?

PRACTICAL APPLICATION

But be doers of the word,
and not hearers only, deceiving yourselves.
— James 1:22

Don't allow anything to distract you from spending time with Jesus.

1. Describe an instance in which you drew upon your spiritual armor to
    change a wrong emotion or attitude.
2. How is prayer significant in your personal life today?
3. How has God most recently responded to you in prayer?

Notes

Notes

_____
_____
_____
_____
_____
_____
_____
_____
_____
_____
_____
_____
_____
_____
_____
_____
_____
_____
_____
_____
_____
_____
_____
_____
_____
_____
_____
_____
_____
_____

CLAIM YOUR FREE RESOURCE!

As a way of introducing you further to the teaching ministry of Rick Renner, we would like to send you FREE of charge his teaching, "How To Receive a Miraculous Touch From God" on CD or as an MP3 download.

In His earthly ministry, Jesus commonly healed *all* who were sick of *all* their diseases. In this profound message, learn about the manifold dimensions of Christ's wisdom, goodness, power, and love toward all humanity who came to Him in faith with their needs.

☑ **YES, I want to receive Rick Renner's monthly teaching letter!**

Simply scan the QR code to claim this resource or go to: **renner.org/claim-your-free-offer**

Connect WITH US!